SCHIRMER'S LIBRARY
OF MUSICAL CLASSICS

Vol. 377

FELIX MENDELSSOHN-BARTHOLDY

Sixteen
Two-Part So[ngs]

T0079168

English Versions by

DR. THEODORE BAKER

and others

G. SCHIRMER, Inc.

DISTRIBUTED BY

HAL•LEONARD®
CORPORATION
7777 W. BLUEMOUND RD. P.O. BOX 13819 MILWAUKEE, WI 53213

CONTENTS.

"I would that my Love."

„Ich wollt', meine Lieb.'"

(H. Heine.)

English version by
Dr. Th. Baker.

F. MENDELSSOHN.

Nº 1.

gäb' ich den lust'-gen Win - den, die__ trü - gen es lu - stig
gay winds would I con - fide__ it, They'd waft it so gai - ly

cresc.

gäb' ich den lust'-gen Win - den, die trü - gen es lu - stig
gay winds would I con - fide__ it, They'd waft it so gai - ly

cresc.

fort, das gäb'__ ich den lust'-gen Win - den, die__
on, To gay__winds would I con - fide it, They'd

f

fort, das gäb' ich den lust'-gen Win - den, die__
on, To gay winds would I con - fide it, They'd

fz *f*

trü - gen es lu - stig fort, es lu - stig fort,____
waft it so gai - ly on, so gai - ly on,____

trü - gen es lu - stig fort, es lu - stig
waft it so gai - ly on, so gai - ly

p *p*

die__ trü - gen es lu - stig fort.
They'd waft it so gai - ly on.

fort,__ die trü - gen es lu - stig fort.
on,__ They'd waft it so gai - ly on.

Sie tra - gen zu dir, __ Ge-
They waft __ it to thee, __ be-

Sie tra - gen zu dir, __ Ge-
They waft __ it to thee, __ be-

lieb - te das lieb- - er - füll - te Wort; du __
lov - ed, From my_____ o'er - flow - ing heart, Thou __

lieb - te das lieb- - er - füll - te Wort; du
lov - ed, From my_____ o'er - flow - ing heart, Thou

Farewell Song of the Birds of Passage.

Abschiedslied der Zugvögel.

(Hoffmann von Fallersleben.)

English version by
Dr. Th. Baker.

F. MENDELSSOHN.

Greeting.
Gruss.
(L.von Eichendorff.)

English version by
Dr. Th. Baker.

F. MENDELSSOHN.

blei - chen, die Lie - be oh - ne Glei - chen bleibt e - wig im Her - zen
per - ish: The love that so I cher - ish Shall nev - er for-sake my

die Lie - be oh - ne Glei - chen bleibt
The love that so I cher - ish Shall

steh'n, _____ bleibt e - wig im Her - zen steh'n, e - wig im Her - zen
heart, _____ shall nev - er for-sake my heart, nev - er for-sake my

e - wig im Her - zen steh'n, e - wig steh'n, e - wig im Her - zen
nev-er for-sake my heart, ne'er for - sake, nev - er for-sake my

steh'n, bleibt e - wig im Her - zen steh'n!
heart, shall nev - er for-sake my heart!

steh'n, bleibt ___ e - wig im Her - zen steh'n!
heart, shall ___ nev - er for-sake my heart!

Autumn Song.
Herbstlied.
(Klingemann.)

English version by
Dr. Th. Baker.

F. MENDELSSOHN.

wan - delt sich al - le die Fröh - lich - keit! Bald sind die
Do all so si - lent and still a - bide? Soon will the

wan - delt sich al - le die Fröh - lich - keit!
Do all so si - lent and still a - bide?

letz - ten Klän - ge ver-flo - gen,
last ___ sweet e - cho be dy - ing,

Bald sind die letz - ten
Soon will the last ___ sweet

Bald ist das letz - te Grün da -
Soon will the last green leaf down -

Sän - ger ge - zo - gen!
song - ster be fly - ing,

Bald! _____
Soon! _____

Süss wie der Lenz, und schnell— ver-weht?
Charm-ing as Spring, ye love thought's vain?

Ei - nes, nur
One thing, there

cresc.

Ei - nes, nur Ei - nes will nim - mer wan - ken:
One thing there is that will nev - er leave me—

cresc.

Ei - nes will nim - mer wan - ken, nur Ei - nes will
is that will nev - er leave me, there's one thing will

p

cresc.

cresc. sempre.

cresc. e ritard.

f

Es ist das Seh - nen, das nim - mer ver-geht.
It is my yearn-ing, 'twill ev - er re-main!

cresc. e ritard.

f

nim - mer wan - ken: Es ist das Seh - nen, das nim-mer ver-geht.
nev - er leave me It is my yearn ing. 'twill ev - er re-main!

f e ritard

"O wert thou in the cauld blast."

(„O säh' ich auf der Haide dort.")

(Burns.)

F. MENDELSSOHN.

schütz' ich dich, be - schütz' ich dich! Und kommt mit sei - nem
shel - ter thee, I'd shel - ter thee! Or did mis - for - tune's

Stur - me je dir Un - glück nah, dir Un - glück nah,
bit - ter storms A - round thee blaw, a - round thee blaw,

dann wär' dies Herz dein Zufluchtsort, gern theilt' ich's ja, gern theilt' ich's ja!
Thy bield should be my bo - som To share it a', to share it a'.

The May-bell and the Flowers.
Maiglöckchen und die Blümelein.

English version by
Dr. Th. Baker.

F. MENDELSSOHN.

lein, die Blü - me - lein.
pale, all, all are pale.

lein, die Blü - me - lein.
pale, all, all are pale.

pp   *cresc.* -

f >

Doch   kaum der Reif das Thal verlässt, da
But   hard - ly was Jack Frost gone by, When

f >

Doch   kaum der Reif das Thal verlässt, da
But   hard - ly was Jack Frost gone by, When

f

ru - fet wie - der schnell Mai - glöckchen zu dem Frühlingsfest und läu-tet doppelt
May-bell call'd a - main, Rang   in the spring right mer - ri - ly, And rang and rang a -

ru - fet wie - der schnell Mai - glöckchen zu dem Frühlingsfest und läu-tet doppelt
May-bell call'd a - main, Rang   in the spring right mer - ri - ly, And rang and rang a -

"I waited for the Lord."

„Ich harrete des Herrn"

from
"Hymn of Praise."

English Paraphrase by
HENRY STEVENS.

F. MENDELSSOHN.

Note: This Duet has in the original an important part for the chorus. It is published in this arranged form merely for chamber use, where the more complete version in unavailable.

Ich
I

Ich har - re-te des Herrn,__ und er neig - te sich__
I wait - ed for the Lord,__ He in - clin - ed un - -

har - re - te des Herrn, und er neig - te sich zu mir, und
wait - ed for the Lord, He in - clin - ed un - to me, And

_ zu mir,_____ und er hör - te mein Fleh'n;
_ to me,_____ And He an - swer'd my cry.

hör - te mein Fleh'n,__ und hör - te mein Fleh'n; Ich
an - swer'd my cry,__ and an - swer'd my cry. I

setzt auf den Herrn, den Herrn._____
trust in the Lord, the Lord._____

Herrn, auf den Herrn, den Herrn._____
Lord, in the Lord, the Lord._____

Ich har - re - te des
I wait - ed for the

Ich har - re - te des Herrn, des_____
I wait - ed for the Lord, the_____

Herrn, des Herrn; er
Lord, the Lord; He in -

Herrn, des Herrn; er neig - te sich zu
Lord, the Lord; He in - clin - ed un - to

neig - te sich zu mir, zu mir,
clin - ed un - to me, to me,

mir,___ er neig - te sich zu mir, Wohl dem,___
me,___ He in - clin - ed un - to me, To me,___

Wohl dem,___ der sei - ne Hoff - nung, sei - ne
To me,___ who put my hope, who put my

der sei - ne Hoff - nung, sei - ne
who put my hope, who put my

Hoff - - nung setzt auf ihn.
hope___ and trust in Him.

Hoff - - nung setzt auf ihn
hope___ and trust in Him.

Ped.

pp

pp

p

"My Song therefore shall be."
(„Drum sing' ich mit meinem Liede.")
from
Hymn of Praise.

English Paraphrase by
HENRY STEVENS.

F. MENDELSSOHN.

dan-ke dir für al - les Gu-te, das___ du an mir ge - than, das___
thanking Thee for all the mer-cy Thou___ un-to me hast shown, Thou___

___ du an mir ge - than; drum sing'ich mit mei - nem
___ un-to me hast___ shown. My song there-fore shall be___

Lie-de dein Lob,___ du treu - er Gott, e - wig, du treu - er
sounding Thy praise,___ Thou faith- ful God, al - way, Thou faith-ful

Und wandl'ich in Nacht und tie - fem Dun-kel, und die Feinde um-her
Tho' wand-'ring in night and deep-est dark-ness, And my en - emies all

Gott.
God.

sempre p

cresc. -

stel - len mir nach, _____ mir nach, und wandl'ich in Nacht, und tie - fem
com-pass me round, _____ all round, Tho' wand-'ring in night and deep - est

f

p

cresc. -

Dun-kel, und die Fein-de um-her stel-len mir nach, die Fein - de
dark-ness, And my en - e-mies all compass me round, all com - pass,

p

cresc.

sf

"For in His own hand."

„Denn in seiner Hand."

From Psalm XCV.

English Paraphrase by
HENRY STEVENS.

F. MENDELSSOHN.

Nº 9.
Piano.

Denn in sei - ner
For in His own

Hand ist, was die Er - de bringt, was die Er - de
hand is what the earth brings forth, what the earth brings

58

"By the plashing fount I stand."

„An des lust'gen Brunnens Rand."

(Goethe.)

English version by
Dr. Th. Baker.

F. MENDELSSOHN.

No 10.
Zuleika.

Allegretto.

1. An des lust' - gen Brun - nens Rand,__ der in
des__ Ca - na - les, der ge-
1. By the plash - ing fount I stand,__ Where the
meets the plain,__ In the

Piano.

Was - ser - fä - - den spielt,__ wusst' ich nicht, was fest mich__
reih - ten Haupt - al - lee,__ blickt' ich wie - der in die__
whirl - ing ed - dies play,__ Hard - ly know - ing why I __
shad - y wood - land way,__ Now a - loft my glanc - es__

hielt. Doch da war__ von dei - ner Hand __ mei - ne
Höh'. Und da sah__ ich a - ber - mals__ mei - ne
stay. But be - low,__ up - on the sand__ Writ by
stray, And I see__ my name a - gain, __ Like a

con fuoco.

Was - ser springend, wal - lend, die Cy - pres - sen dir ge - steh'n: von Su-
wa - ters play-ing, plash-ing, And the trees__ to thee a - vow:__   From Zu-

Zuleika. espress.

Blei - be,
Ah, be

Hassan.   dim.

lei - ka   zu   Su - lei - ka   ist mein Kom-men und mein Geh'n,   von Su-
lei - ka   to   Zu - lei - ka   All my fan - cies   come and go,__   From Zu-

blei - be   mir ge - wo - gen!   blei - be, bleibe mir ge - wo - gen, blei - be,
ev - er   true to   me, love,   Ah, be ev-er true to me, love, Ah, be

lei - ka   zu   Su - lei - ka   ist mein Kom-men und mein Geh'n,   von Su-
lei - ka   to   Zu - lei - ka   All my fan - cies   come and go,   From Zu-

"How can I blithe and cheerful be?"

„Wie kann ich froh und lustig sein?"

English Version by
HENRY STEVENS.

F. MENDELSSOHN.

Andante con moto.

Früh-ling putzt die Bir-ken aus, es— grünt und blüht und lacht—der Mai, dann
flow'rs re-turn with laugh-ing May, The birch-es show their bloom on high, Soon

kehrt er heim, der weit hinaus, dann, dann kehrt er heim, der weit hinaus,
he'll come home who's far— a-way, soon, soon he'll come home who's far— a-way,

dim.
dann kehrt er heim, der weit___ hin-aus.
soon he'll come home who's far___ a-way.

Evening Song.
Abendlied.

English version by
Dr. Th. Baker.

F. MENDELSSOHN.

Andante tranquillo.

Nº 12.
Piano.

1st Voice.

Wenn ich auf dem La - ger lie - ge, in Nacht__ ge - hüllt, so
When, fold-ed in night's dark man - tle, to rest I re - pair, A

2nd Voice.

Wenn ich auf dem La - ger lie - ge, in Nacht__ ge - hüllt, so
When, fold-ed in night's dark man - tle, to rest I re - pair, A

schwebt mir vor ein sü - - - sses, an - muthig liebes Bild, ein
sweet and charming vi - - - sion Be - fore me ris - es there, a

schwebt mir vor ein sü - - sses, an - muthig liebes Bild, ein
sweet and charming vi - - sion Be - fore me ris - es there, a

dim.

"I lean'd against the tow'ring mast."
Wasserfahrt.

English version by
Dr. Th. Baker.

F. MENDELSSOHN.

I weep because they have taken my Lord away.

Tulerunt Dominum meum.

(St. John: XX, 13, 15.)

English paraphrase by
Dr. Th. Baker.

F. MENDELSSOHN.

Copyright, 1896, by G. Schirmer, Inc.

"Now are we Ambassadors."

„So sind wir nun Botschafter."

(From "St. Paul.")

English paraphrase by
Dr. Th. Baker.

F. MENDELSSOHN.

Nº 15.
Soprano Solo.

Piano.

Recitative.

Und Pau - lus kam zu der Ge - mein - de   und pre - dig - te   den
And Saul came to the con - gre - ga - tion   and freely preach'd the

Na - men des Herrn Je - su   frei.   Da sprach der heil'ge Geist: sen - det mir aus   Bar - na - bas und
name of the Lord Je - sus Christ. Then said the Ho - ly Ghost: Sep - a - rate me   Bar - na - bas and

Pau - lus zu dem Werk, da - zu ich sie be - ru - fen ha - be.   Da fas - te - ten sie und
Saul_ for the work, the work where - un - to I have call'd them.   And when they had pray'd and

be - te - ten,   und leg - ten die Hän - de auf sie   und lies - sen sie gehen._
fast - ed,   they laid their_ hands_ on them   and sent them a - way._

"For so hath the Lord commanded."

„Denn also hat uns der Herr geboten:"

from

"St. Paul."

English paraphrase by
Dr. Th. Baker.

F. MENDELSSOHN.

88

Herrn _____ wird an - ru-fen, der soll se - lig, se - lig wer -
name _____ of the Lord shall be for ev - er, ev - er bless -

Herrn _____ wird an - ru-fen, der soll se - lig, se - lig wer -
name _____ of the Lord shall be for ev - er, ev - er bless -

den, der soll se_lig wer _ _den.
ed, yea, for ev_er bless_ _ed.

den, der_ soll se_lig_ wer _ _den.
ed, yea,_ for ev_er_ bless_ _ed.